ISBN 978-1-331-69716-9
PIBN 10222873

English
Français
Deutsche
Italiano
Español
Português

www.forgottenbooks.com

Mythology Photography **Fiction**
Fishing Christianity **Art** Cooking
Essays Buddhism Freemasonry
Medicine **Biology** Music **Ancient
Egypt** Evolution Carpentry Physics
Dance Geology **Mathematics** Fitness
Shakespeare **Folklore** Yoga Marketing
Confidence Immortality Biographies
Poetry **Psychology** Witchcraft
Electronics Chemistry History **Law**
Accounting **Philosophy** Anthropology
Alchemy Drama Quantum Mechanics
Atheism Sexual Health **Ancient History**
Entrepreneurship Languages Sport
Paleontology Needlework Islam
Metaphysics Investment Archaeology
Parenting Statistics Criminology
Motivational

The Saints and Servants of God.

THE

LIFE OF ST. AGNES

OF ROME.

VIRGIN AND MARTYR.

TRANSLATED FROM THE FRENCH.

PUBLISHED WITH THE APPROBATION OF
THE RIGHT REV. BISHOP OF PHILADELPHIA.

PHILADELPHIA:
PUBLISHED BY PETER F. CUNNINGHAM.

Entered according to the Act of Congress, in the year 1856, by
PETER F. CUNNINGHAM,
In the Office of the Clerk of the District Court of the Eastern
District of Pennsylvania.

S. DOUGLAS WYETH, AGT., STEREOTYPER.
No 7 Pear Street, Phila.

LIFE OF ST. AGNES, OF ROME

INTRODUCTION.

THREE centuries were gone by since the blood of Jesus Christ had flowed upon Calvary, and the blood of Christians, meanwhile, was flowing continually, without other cessation than that occasioned from time to time by the weariness of the executioners. Still, however, the Gospel had penetrated even to the extremities of the earth. Christianity had transformed millions of souls; a new world was about to go forth as from a new creation; it seemed but to await a last moistening dew of the blood of martyrs in order to burst into existence. The time was approaching, in fine, when the ransom of the world would be complete; one, and the last installment, so to speak, remained to be paid, and the redeemed world would belong openly to Christ.

But the temples of the false gods, although empty of worshippers, were still standing. " The prince of this world" * there held sovereign power, and never had the satanic character of that power appeared more formidable. The Roman empire, like the scarlet beast foretold by St. John, had seven heads, which bore as many names of blasphemy.† She lifted them all up, at the same time, against Christ and against his Church, and began a deadly contest, a gigantic and desperate combat. Then arose that great persecution, the most formidable and cruel that had yet embrued the church in blood, and which has been called the era of martyrs. The earth was deluged with the blood of Christians, and the emperors already flattered themselves

NOTES:

* This expression was familiar to St. John by which to designate the demon: Nune princess, etc.

† The Empire, about this epoch, had, in fact, seven emperors, Augustuses or Caesars, who, for the most part, bore as a sign of apotheosis, names borrowed from the false gods—such as Diocletian *Jovius*, Maximian *Hercules*, Galerius son of *Mars*, etc

that they had annihilated even their very name. Witness those famous inscriptions* wherein these masters of the world published their supposed victory. But they who vainly imagined they had put an end to the religion of Christ, have seen but the end of their own power and life. The trophy of the defeat of the Christians became that of their triumph. The seven heads of the monster were struck off, one after another, and there was a song of victory in heaven and upon earth.

And what prodigies of holy heroism shone out among the children of the church!

Innumerable athletes rose up for the battle of the Lord in all ranks of society, of both sexes, of all ages. And the Lord, as though to reject no sacrifice, and to associate the various conditions of life in the divine work of redemption, was pleased to choose everywhere indiscriminately his witnesses: the senator and

NOTES:

*Cluniae in Hispania, in nobile columna haec inscriptio legitur: Diocletian, etc. (Baronius.)

tl ᵕ , ᵕ ave, the matron and the servant, the old man and the child were called to fill up, by mar tyrdom, what was yet wanting to the passion of Christ.*

No church then offered more illustrious sacri- fice than the church of Rome, mother and mis- tress of all the others. It is one of her most glorious recollections, one of her most touching memories which we now propose to relate.

NOTES :

* Qui nune gaudeo in passionibus pro vobis, etc. (Co loss —1 24.)

LIFE OF ST. AGNES, OF ROME.

VIRGIN AND MARTYR.

ABOUT the year of Christ 303, there lived in Rome a young girl born of parents illustrious in the world by their nobility, but more illustrious in the church on account of their sanctity.

Faith was already an inheritance for many families, in which the ancient Roman nobility was soon to be effaced and lost.

This maiden was called Agnes, * a name which signifies *lamb* in Latin and *chaste* in Greek. As a presage of martyrdom and title of innocence, it seemed to indicate the future in her regard.† Indeed, she admirably fulfilled the meaning in its double acceptation, by the meekness of a lamb of sacrifice, as well as by the

NOTES:

* Agnes latinè Agnam significat, etc.
† Ut mihi videatur, etc. (S. Ambrose.)

lustre of her chastity. Thus many of the holy fathers do not mention her name without praising its beautiful conformity to her life, and proclaiming her the justly titled.*

In age, Agnes still bordered on childhood, being only thirteen or fourteen years old when quitting death she found life, † having loved the sole Author of life; but her wisdom and prudence were those of mature age.

Other virtues were very early remarked in Agnes, besides her innocence and meekness: educated at the school of Jesus Christ and in the science of the saints, she manifested in her tender years, that ardent zeal for the salvation of others, which has ever been the passion of a soul where love and faith abound. The Greek Menaea, confirmed besides by other testimony, made known to us ‡ that she gathered together many persons of her own sex, to instruct them

NOTES

* Vitam ea nomini convenienter instituebat.
† Mortem perdidit, etc.
‡ Multas ad se convenientes etc.

in the word of truth—to teach them to know Jesus Christ and to adore him alone. *

God is often pleased to entrust his praise to the lips of childhood, and the Scriptures tell us that it becomes thereby more perfect. † What indeed more worthy of the Divinity, than truths the holiest and the highest, gushing out from a youthful heart replete with grace and innocence, as from a limpid fountain! Thus the child Jesus taught the astonished doctors in the temple. Humble neophytes came then in crowds to gather the words of life from the lips of a child, and doubtless they regarded this as a new prodigy in that religion of prodigies.

We see thus that amidst persecution, and despite the edicts of emperors, all the customs of the Christian life were followed, even by women and children; nothing could prevail against the fervor of souls, to which the interior voice of grace had spoken.

NOTES:

* Ad S.—Agnetem fideles convenisse, etc.

† Ex ore infantium et lactentium perfecisti lauaem tuam, (Psal.—VIII. 3.)

One day as Agnes was returning from an as-
sembly of this kind, * the son of the prefect
of Rome saw her, and struck by her beauty,
fell desperately in love with her. This young
man was named Procopius.† He inquired after the parents of Agnes, and went to ask her
in marriage, his hands full of presents and prom-
ising others still more valuable.

But the young Christian rejected as vile
objects the precious ornaments which he had
brought; still the passion of the unhappy man
was yet more inflamed. Seeing his proposal and
his gifts refused, he supposed that still richer

NOTES:

* Quae dam a scholis reverteretur—This expression
(from the schools) used in the Acts, would seem to be a
new confirmation of the circumstance related by the Menaea.
It is not probable, indeed, that it was secular instruction,
which Agnes went to seek in those schools. All other
knowledge but that of Jesus Christ was vain in the eyes
of the first Christians. Agnes, at fourteen years of age,
had her heart and soul replenished with this knowledge,
and it was rather to teach those who were still ignorant of
it than to learn herself that she frequented those schools.

† S. Adelmar hune adolescentem Procopium vocat, (Bollandus.)

jewels might move Agnes, and hastened **to se-**
lect, from his precious stones, **all** the most brilliant and rare.

Having in vain renewed his efforts, he brought
his relations and friends to the young girl that
they might endeavor to overcome her repug-
nance. These promised her riches, a palace,
estates, numerous slaves, and all the delights
of life if she would consent to a marriage with
Procopius.

The circumstances of this interesting scene
are indicated to a certain point by the replies of
Agnes, which have been handed down to us,
in all their native simplicity; an idea, likewise,
may be formed of the various inducements offered to her, although the Acts have not preserved
the profane discourses of the Pagans. The language of the young girl, enthusiastic, and impas-
sioned, sufficiently demonstrates the character
of a conversation, one side of which has been
withheld. It is shown by the broken sentences,
the words so abundant and diffuse, and above all
by the repetition, which seem to have been pro-

voked by reiterated and earnest entreaties. We will suppress nothing of that vivid imagination nor of those outpourings of affection, which sparkle and burn in the words of the youthful affianced bride of the mystic Spouse.

To the young man, whose importunities made discord with the pious affections of her heart, and alarmed her tender innocence, she said: * "Begone from me, fuel of sin, nourishment of vice, food of death; begone from me, for already a lover has secured my heart; he has given me ornaments more precious than yours, and has placed his ring upon my finger as a pledge of fidelity. He is incomparably more noble than you, both in origin and dignity. He has been pleased to adorn my right hand with a priceless bracelet, and to encircle my neck with diamonds. He has set in my ears rings of peerless pearl and has girdled me with precious stones dazzling as the light of the sun in spring. My Beloved has

NOTES:

* Ad haec beata Agnes tale fertur juveni dedisse responsum: "Discede a me," etc. All the Latin quotations given without a name, are taken from the Acts.

placed his sign upon my forehead, that I may recognise no lover but himself. He has clothed me in golden tissue and adorned me with innumerable ornaments." Again—"He has shown me countless treasures, of which he has promised me the possession, if I remain faithful to him. Could I then so wrong my first love as to accept another and abandon him to whom I am united by the most ardent affection!"

By such sensible images, Agnes meant to symbolize the spiritual ornaments and treasures of grace with which Baptism had adorned and enriched her soul, and which Jesus Christ promised still further to increase in recompense of her virginity. But the Pagans, who heard her words without comprehending their signification, could only discern in them the illusions and dreams of a young girl, bewildered by her imagination. In this view they spoke of a happiness more real, and perhaps even expressed some doubt regarding the perfections of her mysterious Spouse. Agnes then, with still more

2

vivacity, resumed:* "Yes, he is far nobler, his power is greater, his aspect more charming in my sight, his love sweeter to my heart, his grace, in a word, more ravishing than anything to which he could possibly be compared. His voice like a melting harmony enchants my ears. Virgins—my companions—cease not to sound his praise, and such is his beauty, that the sun and the stars behold it amazed. His ministers are angels, who are eager to serve him. At his touch the sick are healed; the dead are awoke by the odor of his virtue. His resources never fail, his riches never decrease. He has already prepared a dwelling for me. I have pledged my faith, I have vowed to be entirely his. Milk and honey flow from his lips. I have felt his chaste embrace. His body was united to mine, and "the blood from his stricken cheek has impressed itself on mine." But know that his mother was a virgin—that he was begotten by the Father

NOTES :

* Lujus generositas celsior, possibilitas fortior, aspectus pullelvot amer suavior etc.

from all eternity. I can love him and remain chaste; press him to my heart and rest pure, receive him as my Spouse and still be a virgin. And the children of this union will be brought forth without pain; their number will increase and multiply."

By these last words, Agnes evidently alluded to those souls whom she was to bring forth to the faith, and to nourish with the word of life.

The passion of Procopius still increased.— His body so suffered from the anguish of his mind, that he, at length, lay prostrate upon a bed of sickness. His profound sighs betrayed the nature of his malady to the physicians in attendance, who delayed not to inform his father of it.

The prefect, whose name was Symphronius, renewed in person all his son's entreaties in order to gain the consent of the young virgin.— Agnes again refused, saying that nothing in the world could make her violate the fidelity she had vowed to her first love. Symphronius replied that, as he was invested with the prerog-

atives of power, no person—however illustrious
he might be—could be considered a better
alliance than the one proposed. He, however,
failed not to inquire carefully concerning the
Spouse whose power Agnes had so greatly laud-
ed. One of his courtiers informed him that the
young girl was a Christian, addicted, like the
rest, to magical arts, and called Christ her
Spouse.

The prefect was rejoiced to receive this intel-
ligence, and summoned Agnes, with great ceremony. before his tribunal. He was aware, in
fact. that he had thus become the arbiter of her
destiny. In an accusation of christianity none
dared present themselves to defend her cause.
Besides, what defence was possible, when the
accused, far from palliating her crime, gloried in
it, and renewed it publicly in presence of the
judge? He who should have pleaded her innocence, would have raised against himself the
prince, the priests, and the people, and, from
being an advocate, would have himself become
the accused. The prefect understood then that

neither the relations of Agnes, nor the Roman nobility of which they formed a part, would dare to accompany her to his tribunal in order to protect her cause.

He began by addressing himself to Agnes in particular, hoping to prevail over her by sweet words, and by appearing to act rather as a friend than as a judge ; but persuasion having failed, he employed menaces. The firmness of the virgin of Christ was no more shaken by his denunciations of impending evil, than seduced by his promises, and, with the same unchanged expression, she smiled both at flatteries and threats. * Symphronius seeing such great intrepidity in one so young, turned to her parents. As they were of the nobility he dared not employ violence against them, but menaced them with an accusation of christianity. It is known that before such a charge fell all the privileges of rank, even the title of citizen, of which the Romans were so jealous. The slave was still

NOTES :

* Sed Christi virgo nec blandimentis seducitur, etc.

something in society : " a second human kind,"
as the historian Florus says ;* there existed
laws which regulated his lot, and in a certain
degree, protected his person.   For the Christian
there was neither rank in the world, nor a place
in heaven ; for him there was but one law :—
that of proscription.

Meanwhile, the prefect detained Agnes.   The
following day, he caused her to be again brought
into his presence, and repeated what he had already said of his son, of his passion, and his
desires.   Agnes simply replied :† " I pray you
injure not my Spouse by supposing that I could
allow myself to be seduced from him by your
promises.   My life belongs to him who has chosen me the first."

For a third time, the young virgin was cited
before the prefect, who, seeing that all his words
had been without effect, said :‡ I perceive that

NOTES:

* Per fortunam in omnia obnoxii quasi secundum hominum genus sunt, (Florus III. 20).

† At illa : " Haec sponsi injuria, etc.

‡ Cui et dixit : " Superstitio Christianorum," etc.

you will not have done with your folly, nor will you lend an ear to the counsels of wisdom until your heart is torn from the Christian superstition, whose wicked arts you practice. You are going then to be consecrated to the worship of the goddess Vesta, so that if you are determined to preserve your virginity, you may, at least, devote it to watching day and night at her august altars."

Agnes replied:* "If I have refused a union with your son, who although under the dominion of an insensate passion, is, at least, a living man, endowed with understanding, capable of seeing, feeling, and walking; who enjoys the light of day in common with the good; if, for the love of Jesus Christ, nothing has been able to persuade me to listen to him, how could I vow to serve a deaf and dumb idol, destitute of feeling and of life? how could I so outrage the supreme God as to bow my head before a vain bit of stone?

NOTES :

* Ad hæc beata Agnes dixit : " Si filium tuum, etc."

" I wish still,* said Symphronius, to take into consideration your extreme youth ; and to excuse your blasphemies against the gods, since yours is not the age of reason. But have more regard for your own safety than thus to expose yourself to the anger of the gods."

" Set aside," resumed Agnes, " this pity for my youth, and think not that I wish to make use of such a plea in order to gain your indulgence.— Faith resides not in the years of time, but in the sentiments of the heart, and the all powerful God considers rather the state of our soul than the length of our life. As to your gods, whose anger you fear on my account, leave them to their rage; let them make themselves heard ; let them order that they shall be vererated, and command that they shall be adored. But since you will never obtain the object of your desires. carry out your intention without delay."

At this unshaken firmness and courageous de- fiance the prefect could contain himself

NOTES:

* Audiens haec Symphronius praefectus dixit: Cu etc.

longer, and cried out:* "You think by the contempt of torments and the disdain of a life, which you regard as worthless, to escape punishment; but to inflict it. know, that I will take advantage of that modesty, which is so dear to you, of that virginity, which you have reserved for your God. Choose then† either to sacrifice to the goddess Vesta, with the virgins consecrated to her altar, or to be sent to a public brothel. Far‡ from you will then be all those Christians, who have imbued you with their magic, and for whose presence, in your anguish, you will vainly long to strengthen and uphold your courage. The sentence, in fine, is pronounced:§ for the honor of your family sacrifice to Vesta. or, to the shame of your parents, become a lost woman, an object of public scorn."

" Not so,"‖ Agnes answered; "Christ forgets

NOTES

* Si facile est, ait, etc. (Prudentius.)
† Unum tibi de duobus elige: etc.
‡ Longè erunt á te Christiani, etc.
§ Unde, ut dixi, aut sacrifica deae Vestae, etc.
‖ Haud, in qrit Agnes, immemor est ita Christus etc.

not his own; never will he abandon to destruc-
tion that modesty so precious in his sight.   He
is ever present to aid the pure.   He will not
suffer a blemish to the honor of my virginity.—
Over this you have no power, although you may
stain your sword in my blood.   I know * the
omnipotence of Jesus Christ my Lord; I trust
in him and despise your threats, confident that
I shall neither sacrifice to your idols, nor suffer
any harm.   For the Lord has placed his angel
near me to be my protector, and the Son of the
true God, whom you know not, is my rampart
and my defence; he will never fail me.   Your
gods,† on the contrary, are made of brass,
fitter for fashioning utensils for the use of man,
or of stone, which would better serve to pave
the public way.   No, the Divinity resides not
in a senseless stone, but dwells in heaven; it is
not brass or other metal that constitutes a God;
it is sovereign power, it is omnipotence.   Know

NOTES:

* Unde eqo quia novi virtutem Domini mei, etc.

† Du autem tui aut ærei sunt ex quibus cucumae me-
‿us fiunt ad usus hominum, etc.

then, you and all those who imitate you, that if you forsake not the worship of idols, a fate like unto theirs is reserved for you. For even as they have been moulded by fire, so their adorers will burn in flames, not to be cast into form, but to be destroyed and to perish forever."

At these words the iniquitous judge ordered that she should be despoiled of her garments and then led to a place of infamy, preceded by the public crier, proclaiming that :* Agnes, a sacreligious virgin and blasphemer of the gods, was condemned to the lupanar."

At the moment† the first part of this sen- tence was executed, the long tresses of Agnes unbraided themselves, and, by a prodigy of divine grace, took suddenly such a wondrous growth, that, (encircling her whole person) she was better concealed by them than by her own garments.

NOTES :

* Aguem virginem sacrilegam, etc.

† Statim autem ut expotiata est, crine resolute, tantam densitatem, etc.

Agnes was thus led to the Agonale Circus,* where stood those places of turpitude, † as the Acts, in their chaste language, designated them. What a time was that when such a sentence could be pronounced by the first magistrate of Rome, and executed in the capital of the civilized world, without exciting public indignation ! ‡ However, Prudentius relates § that the crowd

NOTES

* The Agonale Circus was built on the site of the great circus of Tarquin the elder. Places stained with so much blood and crime, became (after Agnes had purified them by her presence) the abodes of holiness and prayer. The piety of the faithful led them eagerly to visit those infamous vaults (fornices) which had been transformed into a sanctuary. When, in the course of time, they had fallen into ruin. pope Callixtus II, in 1123, obeying that voice of veneration, which still remained unweakened, erected a church on the ruins, which Innocent X, in the 17th century, replaced by a magnificent temple, which exists at this day in the place Navone. (See the description of the Agonale Circus in the Antiga—Romaines d' Andréae Fulvius liv IV. ch. 18).

† In locum turpitudinis, etc.

‡ Le poéte Juvénal, en enumerant les vices de cette Rome dègènerèe. constate cette atrocitè de jeunes filles condamnèes par jugement à la prostitution : Jam pudem, etc,

§ Stantem refugit moesta frequentia, etc.

turned away their eyes and in sadness dis-
persed. But such timid disapprobation was
far removed from those generous transports of
the ancient Romans—the avengers of the chastity of Lucretia and Virginia.

Having arrived at those places of turpitude,
the Christian virgin there found the angel of
the Lord prepared to defend her.* He surrounded her with a dazzling light, whose brilli-
ancy allowed no one to approach or even to see
her. The spot on which she stood shone as the
sun in its mid-day splendor, and the more the
curious eye endeavored to penetrate it, the more
its vision was obscured.

Agnes prostrated herself before the Lord,
and when she had prayed, saw near her a robe
of brilliant whiteness,† with which she clothed
herself, exclaiming: " Thanks be to thee, O
Jesus Christ, my Lord, who hast received me into the number of thy servants, and hast sent me
this garment !"

NOTES :

* Angelum Domini illic præparatum invenit ; etc.
† Apparuit ante oculos, etc.

This robe was so perfectly fitted to her person,* and was of a beauty so extraordinary that
nobody doubted its having been brought by
angels and prepared by their hands.

Meanwhile the lupanar had become a place of
prayer;† all those present, struck with fear
and wonder, rendered honor to the miraculous
light, and withdrew more pure than when they
had entered there.

There was one exception, however, the son of
the prefect, who reproaching the others as weak
cowards,‡ dared to approach the young virgin
rudely. But instantly an angel struck him with
—as it were—lightening from heaven. He fell
with his face to the earth, and palpitating in the
dust, expired, smothered by the demon. Prudentius says that he was struck with blindness only, and lay half dead.§ One of his vicious com-

NOTES

* Ita namque ad mensuram, etc.
† Interca lupanar locus orationis, etc.
‡ Cocpit impotentes arguere, etc.
§ En ales ignis fulminis, etc.

panions entering, and seeing him thus prostrated, cried out: "Come on, friends* come on,
Romans, you who fear the gods, the courtesan
has killed the son of the prefect by her wicked
sorceries!"

Some drew near but quickly retreated, exclaiming: "O power of Christ!† O prodigy of
the Christian's, faith! Meanwhile Agnes was
glorifying, in hymns of praise, her God and Saviour, by whom her virginity had triumphed in
such fearful peril, and through whom the lupanar
even had become an inviolate sanctuary.

Soon a great concourse of people hastened
towards the circus, and expressions of various
import were uttered by the excited multitude;
some exclaiming: "She is a sorceress!" others: "She is a sacrilegious wretch!" again:
"She is an innocent girl!"‡

NOTES:

* Pessimi Romani succunite, etc.

† Magna fides Christianorum! Magna Christi potentia!

‡ Alii dicebant magnam, alii innocentum, alii sacrilegam
conclamabant. One cannot without astonishment see
witchcraft attributed to a young girl, whose "age was not

The prefect, on learning what had happened, hurried, in great affliction, to the place. A piercing shriek escaped him on beholding the body of his son extended motionless upon the ground,

that of reason," to use the words of the prefect himself. Assuredly the miracles which Agnes had wrought, and which attested a supernatural power, were well calculated to make the Pagans believe that she possessed magical arts. But even before she had manifested her miraculous power —considering only her rejection of Procopius and consecration of her virginity to Christ--they had imputed evil practices to her. Was the faith she professed the sole cause of this? No---for we see that all Christians were not indiscriminately charged with the same crime, although their religion, so full of mysteries and wonders was regarded as infected with sorcery. Why then was Agnes, of such tender age, accused of magic rather than the other Christians? We may be allowed to hazard some conjectures in reference to this, which may not be entirely without foundation. The young Christian's contempt of a brilliant union, in order that she might remain a virgin, perhaps first gave rise to this idea of her dealing with evil spirits. Virginity, among the nations of antiquity, was always looked upon as something wonderful and extraordinary, which elevated those who had made such a vow far above nature. To this might be added the singular beauty of Agnes, the effects of which had just been so striking. The beautiful bears within its lf a certain character favorable to superstition; it so impresses the beholders with respect, astonishment, and an indescribable mixture of ven

and turning to the young virgin: *"O! most cruel of women," said he, " by wha, charri have you destroyed my son ? You have chosen him for the victim of your magical arts!" In such words, a thousand times repeated, he reproached her with the death of his son. Agnes replied: "It is the demon,† whose inspirations he fol. lowed, who has received power over his life.— Why have all the others, who had the same intention, escaped a similar fate? It is because they gave honor to God, who sent his angel to my rescue. This angel has clothed me with a robe of mercy, and has protected my person, of-

NOTES :

eration and fear that it has been, regarded as divine. All the celebrated sorceresses, the pythonesses, etc., are represented to us with the double attributes of beauty and virginity. Thus the ancients, with the exception of the Orientals, rarely attributed magic to men ; the middle ages whose genius was different---have alone spoken of old sorceress. They exchanged, in these types of superstition, extreme beauty for extreme ugliness, because it was always under a repulsive exterior that they personified the demon and his works, in whatever way manifested

* Crudelissima omnium feminarum, in filium meum voluisti, etc.

† Ille, cujus voluntatem volebat perficere, etc.

fered and consecrated to Christ from the cradle.
Those, who, seeing the heavenly light, gave
honor to God, have been suffered to depart
unharmed and uninjured. But he, who, not-
withstanding this manifestation, dared to approach me, has been struck by the angel of the
Lord and suffers the penalty which you behold.'
" I will believe,"‡ said the prefect, " that no ne-
cromancy has done this, if you supplicate your
angel to restore my son to life."

"Although your faith," replied Agnes, " is not
worthy to obtain such a miracle from God, yet
as the time has come to manifest the divine
power of Jesus Christ, my Lord, let all go away
that I may speak to him in prayer." When all
had withdrawn, she prostrated herself upon the
ground, and with tears, implored of Heaven,
the life of the young man. Suddenly a new
breath of life reanimated him, his eyes opened
to the light, and he went forth crying out with

NOTES:

‡ In hoc apparebit quia non magicis artibus ista ges-
sisti. etc.

a loud voice : " There is but one God in heaven, on earth, in the whole universe ; He is the God of the Christians ! all our temples are vain all the gods adored in them are vain ! and vain as themselves is the aid expected from them."

The numerous witnesses* of this miracle, were struck with astonishment and fear. Many of them, with the prefect himself, exclaimed : " O ! power of the Christains' faith ! The God of the young virgin is great !" But there were not wanting impious men—men with impure hearts, who revolted at these acclamations. The soothsayers † and the priests of the temples were troubled, and exciting the people, they raised up a sedition among them. But one voice was heard : " Seize the sorceress ! away with the worker of enchantments, who troubles the minds of the people, and perverts their souls !"

NOTES :

* Obstupuerunt universi ad in usitatem hoc prodigium, etc. (Ex Menocis).

† Omnes aruspices et templorum pontifices conturbantur, etc.

Such was,* says Prudentius, the first step oy which Agnes ascended towards her heavenly home; she was full soon to mount others.

At the sight of so many prodigies, the pre-feet remained stupified.† But he was of the number of those men, in whom, (like Pontius Pilate in the trial of our Lord) ambition, or a pusillanimous fear overrules every generous in-stinct, and silences the voice of duty, as well as of gratitude. In view of the edicts of proscrip-tion, he dared not defend Agnes against the sentence, which he had himself pronounced, nor repress the tumult excited by the priests of the temples. He left, then, to his lieutenant As-pasius the task of quelling the sedition, and retired full of sorrow at not being able to deliver her, who had rescued his son from death, and whom he had himself plunged into this extreme danger.

The lieutenant, finding himself strong in the

NOTES :

* Primum sed Agnes hunc habuit gradum, etc.
† Præfectus autem videns tante mirabilia, obstupuit.

weakness of the prefect. became, in consequence perhaps, violent beyond measure. In order to satisfy both the people and the priests, he caused a great fire to be lighted on the public place, into which he ordered Agnes to be thrown. The flames dividing into two parts,* darted out on the right and left against the rioters, whom they burned; not touching the blessed Agnes who was in the middle of the pile. But far from attributing this miracle to divine power, the people saw in it only the effect of magic, and foaming with rage, they clamored towards heaven, Agnes, still encircled by the flames, extending her arms, typified the triumphant sign of the cross, and poured forth the following prayer: †"All powerful God, alone to be adored, alone to be feared, Father of Jesus Christ, our Lord, I bless thee! because, through thine only Son. thou hast saved me from the threats of those impious men, and from

NOTES:

* Statim in duas partes divisæ sunt flammæ, etc.
† Omnipotens, adorande, colende, temende Pater, etc.

defilement while treading the foul places of the demon. Behold now, by thy Holy Spirit, I am penetrated as with a celestial dew. The fire is arrested and dies out before me, while the flames divide and turn against those who kin-dled them. I bless thee, O! Father of glory who hast given me courage to walk intrepidl₊ towards thee even through fire. Behold! what I have believed, I now see!—what I have hoped for, I possess!—what I have desired, I now em-brace!—my lips and my heart confess thee. For thee my inmost being longs. Behold, now to thee I go, the only and true God, who, with thy Son, Jesus Christ, our Lord, and with the Holy Spirit, livest and reignest forever and' ever."

Agnes had hardly finished her prayer, when the fire was so totally extinguished that not even the heat of it remained.

Aspasius, to appease the seditious, whose fury increased every moment, then commanded that she should be beheaded.

The young virgin was loaded with fetters and

cast into the prison of the condemned. But St. Ambrose tell us that her form was so deli- cate, irons could not be found small enough for her arms or neck.* And, indeed, could handcuffs and iron collars ever have been forged for such a tender age? Agnes, motionless under their weight, looked upon them as ornaments. These were, doubtless, the necklace and the bracelets, which her Spouse had promised her. She well knew their value, and felt herself amply com- pensated for the far less precious jewels, which she had refused.

The spectators wept around her; Agnes alone was tearless.† They were astonished to behold one, who had, as yet, scarcely tasted life, throw that life away as if she had exhausted all its sweetness. Not knowing death, she was ready to accept it. But if not ripe for punishment, she was mature for victory. "O detestable cruelty! cries out St. Ambrose, which spares not

NOTES:

* Nunc ferratis colla manusque ambas in serere nexibus; etc.

† Flere omnes, ipsa sine fletu   Mirari plerqiue quod, etc.

such a tender child! But greatness and power of faith, which finds its triumph in such years! The people were amazed to see so courageous a con- fessor of Christ in a child, who could scarcely have had a knowledge of herself. In a word, she made those believe in God, who could not sup pose that she had much human wisdom. But does not that which surpasses nature come from the Author of nature?"

In the meanwhile, the executioner presented himself sword in hand,* At this fearful sight, Ag- nes exclaimed in a transport of joy: "Oh! what a happiness! it is a fierce and barbarous man who now approaches me. Draw near—I prefer your terrible countenance to that of those im- passioned young men who lately threatened me. See, I acknowledge it, behold the suitor whom I love. Come then!—I will go myself to meet you, not restraining the ardent desire which draws me towards you. Strike—behold my breast; I want your sword to penetrate even to

NOTES:

* Ut vidit Agnes stare trucem virum, etc.

the bottom of my heart. Spouse of Christ! it is thus that I shall escape from the darkness of earth and rise to the abode of light. Open oh! all-powerful God, open the gates of heaven, until lately closed to man! O! Christ Jesus draw my soul to thyself—a victim first to thee by virginal consecration, now to thy Father by martyrdom's immolation!"

Saying these words, Agnes sprang towards the block, her heart more joyful, her step quicker than the young bride who goes to her nuptials.* There she stopped—then bowed down her head to adore Jesus Christ, and to receive the stroke of death. The executioner, at the moment of carrying out the atrocious sentence, was so agitated, that he appeared himself to be the condemned; he was pale, and his hand trembled as if threatened by some strange peril, while the young virgin intrepidly awaited the fatal blow.

At length the ardent wish of Agnes was ful-

NOTES:

* Non sic ad thalamum nupta properaret.

4

filled :* the executioner severed her head from her body by a single stroke. So prompt a death prevented the sensation of pain, and the enfranchised soul arose towards heaven. The angels received her on her way, which was marked by a shining track.

It was thus that Christ consecrated to himself as spouse and martyr, the blessed Agnes, cover- ed with the purple of her blood. †

Prudentius, the poet of the glorious combats of the athletes of Christ, having represented the young martyr in her contests, presents her before us in her triumphs also. He delights in following her by that luminous track, which, he supposes, was left behind her in the boundless space.

Agnes,‡ says he, sees, in passing the terres- trial globe at her feet, and casts a last look up- on the darkness from which she is flying. She

NOTES:

* At ille tantam spem, etc.
† Hoc exitu, roseo sui sanquinis,
‡ Miratur orbem subpedibus, etc.

thrills with joy, she is in wonder at the sight of the sun moving in his orbit, with the planets revolving round him. She smiles with pity in beholding the turmoil of human existence, and the rapid flight of time, which carries away with it, kings, tyrants, empires, the pageantry of wealth and honours, which swell the heart with vanity. She regards with compassion that thirst for gold and silver, which, like a raging fever, consumes mortals, and pushes them on to every species of crime. She, pitying looks down upon palaces—mean abodes they seem, erected at so great a cost; upon the vanity of " purple and fine linen." She grieves, so to speak, over the hatreds, the fears, the desires, the continual dangers of earth: its sorrows so long enduring, its joys so rapid in their flight; over that dark envy, with its lighted fire-brand, which withers every hope and tarnishes all human glory; and lastly, she sorrowfully considers the dark night of Gentile superstition, which appears to her worse than all other evils.

She tramples beneath her feet all these

things; she triumphantly places her heel upon the head of that cruel dragon, who sullies with his venom both earth and hell. The foot of a virgin again becomes fatal to him, and plants itself upon his inflamed crest. Vanquished, humbled, he dares no longer raise his head.

Meanwhile, the Most High encircled the brow of Agnes with two immortal crowns, in recompense of martyrdom and virginity: one glowing with sixty rays of light, and the other resplendent with celestial graces, multiplied a hundred times.* "O happy virgin! O! new glory! O! noble inhabitant of our heavenly country, turn towards our miseries thy gracious countenance adorned with this double diadem. O! thou, to whom the omnipotent God gave power to purify a place of pollution by thy presence alone, let thy chaste eyes rest on me, and I, too, shall be purified. There can be nothing impure where thy looks fall, nothing unchaste where thy steps tread.

NOTES:

* An allusion to the 30 and the 100 grains of wheat spoken of in the Gospel.

The parents of Agnes, in resignirg to God the child whom they had brought up for him, felt no deep anguish of soul. In them faith triumphed over nature, and they hesitated not to sacrifice to the Lord that which they held most precious in the world. But in this sacrifice all was not lost to them. They retained the glorious body of the saint, with its evidence of martyrdom—guarantee of life eternal.

The old law commanded the Jews to fly, as from an unclean thing, the contact of a dead body. But in the new law, the bodies of those who, when in life, were dear to God, are not objects of horror but of love.* "God, beautifully says St. John Chrysostom, has divided the martyrs with us: he has taken their souls and given us their bodies."† These holy bodies are not, indeed, insensible matter: a living power still animates them; there resides in them a sanctifying

NOTES:

* Eorum qui apud Deum vivunt, etc. Constitut. Apostol., lib. vi.

† Deus nobiscum partitus est martyres: etc. (Chrysostom, Homil. xcvii).

grace, which communicates itself to those who approach them.* "Thus are still united those whom immense space separates, thus there is a communion between the living and the dead," to make use of the ancient expression of the Christians of Smyrna.† These sentiments, which have always been held by the church, animated, in a particular manner, the early Christians, and the parents of Agnes were deeply imbued with them.

They bore away, with holy joy, the body of their child, and carried it to an estate which they possessed on the Numentan road. ‡

NOTES:

*Modo vero quisquis ossa martyris attingit, etc.(St.Basil).

† In the second century after Christ, the Christians of the church of Smyrna carried away the body of St. Polycarp, their bishop, after his martyrdom: and in the celebrated letter, which they wrote, on this subject, to the faithful of Philomelia, and which is regarded as one of the most authentic monuments of the nature and antiquity of the veneration for the relics of the saints, they expressed their ardent desire to communicate with the sacred remains of Polycarp. (Euseb. Hist. Eccles).

‡ This road led to Numentan, an ancient town of the Sabines, by the Viminale gate, now that of Pius, pope Pius V. having had it reconstructed.

The glorious martyrdom of the young virgin, which had been the cause of such great excitement among an infidel people, called forth, in the same measure, the enthusiasm of the Christians. They wended their way in immense numbers to the burial place of Agnes, but some Pagans observing the large concourse, laid snares for, and stirred up the populace against them. The faithful fled before this multitude of enemies who were armed and in quick pursuit after them. Many of the Christians, however, were wound ed with stones.

But Emerentiana, the foster-sister of Agnes, a very holy virgin, although still a catechumen, far from flying, intrepidly awaited the approach of the Pagans, and reproached them in these terms: " Miserable men, you wickedly put to death the adorers of the all-powerful God, and to avenge your divinities of stone, you slaugh- ter human innocents !"* Saying these words, she was stoned by the mob, who were furious

NOTES:

* " Superflui, miseri, etc.

at hearing themselves thus addressed. Emer.
entiana was, however, able to reach the tomb
of Agnes, where she gave up her soul to God—
her last breath a prayer. We cannot doubt,*
say the Acts, that her blood served for her baptism, since she fearlessly suffered death, cor.-
fessing God, and defending truth and justice.

On the following night, the parents of Agnes,
accompanied by some priests, returned and
buried the body of the blessed Emerentiana in
the same field where reposed the remains of
their child.

During the time which immediately followed
the martyrdom of Agnes, her whole family,
with many of the faithful, watched assiduously
in prayer at her tomb. While thus engaged in
the silence of night, ‡ they suddenly perceived,
moving along in a luminous cloud, a numerous
band of virgins, clothed in robes of golden tis-

NOTES:

* Unde non dubium est quod in suo sanguine sit bapti-
sata, etc.

† Vident in medio noctis silentio exercitum virginum
etc.

sue. In the midst of them was Agnes, adorned like the rest, and having at her right hand **a** lamb as white as snow.

Seeing this vision they were all struck with fear. At a word from Agnes, those heavenly visitants ceased their motion, when, standing before her parents, she thus spoke: " You see it is not as for one dead that you should weep for me, but rejoice with, and congratulate me, for I have received, with my virgin companions, a shining throne, and I am united in heaven to Him who was, on earth, the object of all my love."

Saying these words, Agnes and her companions proceeded on their upward way.

This vision was publicly proclaimed by all those who had been the witnesses of it. One of them related it some years after to Constantia, daughter of the emperor Constantine. This excellent princess was so afflicted with ulcers that her whole body was covered by them. Hearkening to a pious inspiration, and impelled by a hope of recovering her health, she repaired, one night, to the tomb of the virgin martyr, and, although a Pagan, she prayed, her heart full of confidence and faith.

She soon fell into a sweet sleep, and saw in a dream the blessed Agnes, who encouraged her in these words: * "Be faithful, Constantia, and believe in Jesus Christ, the son of God, thy Saviour, by whom thou art going to be cured of the malady; which afflicts thy body."

At the sound of this voice, Constantia awoke so perfectly cured that not even the least scar was to be seen on her body.

The emperor, her father, and the princes her brothers, seeing her return to the palace entirely healed, were filled with joy. The whole city of Rome celebrated the event: the army, the people all expressed their wonder. The idolatry of the Gentiles was in confusion, and the faith of Christ in triumph and in joy.

Constantine, at the request of his daughter, had

NOTES

* " Constanter age, Constantia. et crede Dominum Jesum Christum," etc.

erected over the tomb of Agnes, a superb basilica which still stands, and which after more
than fourteen hundred years, and notwithstand-
ing many restorations, continues to be one of
the most precious monuments of the first ages
of Christianity. Constantine endowed this
church with considerable revenues, and provid-
ed it with sacred vases, and the most magnificent ornaments.*

Adjoining this edifice, Constantia had a monastery built, which also bears the name of Agnes ;
she there consecrated herself to God, and pass-
ed in it the remainder of her days. A great
number of Roman virgins joined her in this retreat and, following her example, received the
religious veil.

In connection with Constantia's retirement
from the world, there is an interesting circum
stance related in the Acts of the holy martyrs
John and Paul, who were both officers belonging

NOTES :

* The Liber Pontificalis contains a curious enumeration
of these ornaments —See, Baronius, Ann. 324—107, etc.

to the household of Constantia.   This princess,
according to the Acts, had been promised in
marriage to one of Constantine's most illustrious generals, named Gallicanus. The latter had,
by a former marriage, two daughters, Attica
and Arthemia, whom he left with his betrothed
as a pledge of their future union.   But when
the princess, absolved from her promise, was
about to consecrate herself to God, she inspired those two young girls with the same gener-
our resolution, and thus replaced by a spiritual
maternity, the maternity of adoption, which
was to have united her to him.

Gallicanus himself was converted to the faith,
and obtained, some years later, (in 362, under
Julian, the apostate), the crown of martyrdom
—a precious compensation for what he had re-
signed to God.

It was also in this monastery that Constantia hospitably entertained pope Liberius, on
his return from exile, as St. Damasus testifies,
his immediate successor on the chair of St.
Peter.

Since that time continual generations of holy virgins have succeeded each other in this pious retreat, and we can still repeat what was said in happier times than ours, by the author of the Acts of our saint;* "As faith suffers nothing from the stroke of death, a great number of Roman virgins still come to unite themselves to the blessed Agnes, as though present in the body; and animated by her example, they preserve courageously, the treasure of their virginity, believing, with unwavering faith, that in reward of their perseverance, there is reserved for them the palm of eternal victory."

Constantia, after having lived near the tomb of Agnes, wished still to repose there in death. After her, a great number of Christians also aspired to place their mortal remains under the guardianship of a body—secure infallibly of a glorious resurrection.

They dug. then around the venerated tomb,

NOTES:

* Et quia fides damna mortis non patitur, usque in hodiernum, etc.

innumerable grottoes, subterranean or sepul chral chambers; magnificent monuments were erected over them, and thus, by degrees, was formed the famous cemetery of St. Agnes, one of the largest and most celebrated of Christian Rome.*

This tomb of the courageous virgin and illus‧trions martyr, was no less for the living, than as concerned the dead, an object of confidence and veneration. Rome, the city of the saints, Rome, so rich in their sacred relics, regarded the tomb of Agnes as one of her most precious treasures, one of her most tutelary supports, and strangers ran thither in crowds to offer up their petitions and invoke the aid of a power so faithful in miracles.

The church was not content with enshrining in gold the bones of Agnes; at the same time

NOTES:

* The numerous monuments, which this cemetery en‑clo‑es, have been described with extreme care by Bosio and his Latin translator Aringhi, in a learned work entitled La Rome Souterraine). From the point of view of art and faith, they have evoked all the pious memories which sleep in these catacombs.

that she placed them on her altars, she inscribed her name in the canon of the Mass, as representing, with six other saints, the order of virgins in the heavenly host, whom the priest invokes during the holy sacrifice.

Besides this glorious privilege, the church has instituted. in honor of St. Agnes, a double feast, which is celebrated on the 28th January (the eighth day after the commemoration of her martyrdom) in memory of that miraculous apparition when she presented herself before her parents, surrounded by a choir of virgins, clothed in golden tissue, and having at her side a snow white lamb. *

It is also to this circumstance that is referred (as to its rites, and perhaps even as regards its origin, the institution of the pallium, an ornament which the pope gives to the arch-bishops

NOTES :

* It is thus that St. Agnes is always represented in the most ancient paintings, as Nolanus informs us in his Histoire des Saintes Images, (liv. 3, chap. VI). And the Roman liturgy chants in the Mass of the 28th of January, these words: "Stans a dextris ejus Agnus nive candidior."

and bishops of certain privileged sees, and which these prelates wear in form of a collar round the neck and falling over the breast and back.* St. Isidore of Pelusa teaches us its symbolical meaning: "The prelate," says he, "wears it on his shoulders, and it is made of wool and not of linen, because it represents the strayed sheep, whom our Lord carried on his shoulder after having found it. The bishop, who holds the place of Christ and continues his work, shows to all, even by his vestment, that he is the imitator of the great and good Pastor,

NOTES:

* Several authors trace back the origin of the pallium to St. Linus, the immediate successor of St. Peter ; but the first positive document, which states its existence, is a constitution of St. Mark, the pope, a cotemporary of Constantine, founder of the basilica of St. Agnes. This coincidence would lead us to suppose that the origin of the pallium, as well as the rites which accompany it, are connected with the veneration of St. Agnes. But, however it may be, if the custom did not commence with St. Agnes, it has been perpetuated through her. See the constitution of St. Mark, quoted by Baronius, (Ann. 3366), from the book of the Roman Pontiffs. "Hic (Marcus) constituit ut episcopus, etc.

who came to raise up and support the weakness of his flock.''

On the 21st of January, (the feast of St. Agnes), two lambs perfectly white are led in procession in the city of Rome; the pope blesses them from the balcony of his palace as they pass. They are afterwards conducted to the basilica of St. Agnes and offered with great pomp at the altar. Their wool is sent to the religious of the convent, who spin it themselves, and make the pallia out of it.

This interesting ceremony goes back even to the foundation of the basilica erected in honor of her whose name signifies lamb, and whose meekness and innocence proclaimed her title to the appellation. Thus the church consecrates, under the auspices of St. Agnes, one of the most touching symbols of the pastoral dignity.

'From the church of Rome, the devotion to St. Agnes soon spread itself throughout the entire world. St. Jerome informs us that, in his time, it was celebrated in all languages, among all nations, and in all the churches.* The church has guarded this possession of glory through catholic ages, which have all left us monuments of their veneration for our saint. In the middle ages, and at every period, in Rome, throughout Italy, in France and Spain, and in the rest of christendom, numerous churches were placed under her invocation; her name was one of the most popular, and most frequently conferred in baptism, so much does faith seek in names a holy patronage, and endeavor to prevent the name of a child becoming, (as is too often the case in our days even in Christian families) a matter of pure caprice, or of a romantic and unmeaning fancy.

A few words remain to be said concerning the relics of St. Agnes.

Her body has always remained in the basilica on the Numentan road, but her head, which fell under the sword, was carried by pope Honorius

NOTES

* Omnium litteris atque linguis in ecclesiis Agnetis vita laudata est.

1. ﻭ the church of St. John Lateran, and is, at present, in that of the Holy Saviour ad sculas.

About the year 1620, under the pontificate of Paul V., the cardinal, Paul Emile Sfondrate, in repairing the grand altar of the Constantine Basilica, discovered there the body of St. Agnes, near that of St. Emerentiana. The head, indeed, was wanting, and the bones were those of a child of the age of Agnes, when she suffered martyrdom. Paul V. replaced these relics with honor under the alter. It appears, however, that they were divided, since one of her arms, together with a finger, are venerated in the church of St. Peter, of the Vatican, and other of her relics in that of St. Mary Major. The French church of St. Louis also preserves a part of her clothing, and the convent of St. Martha, near the Roman college, a part of her girdle. In the Christian world, a large number of other Churches deem themselves also the happy possessors of the bones of St. Agnes

Since the middle of the 10th century, there are relics bearing her name, honored with particular veneration at Utrecht, in Holland. Several historians relate that they were given in Rome, in the year 966, by the sovereign pontiff, to Baldricus, the fifteenth bishop of Utrecht, at the request of Otho I., emperor and king of the Romans. A part of these last relics were afterwards divided between a great number of churches; among others, that of Cologne, of Anvers, of Brussells, and, in 1545, the abbey of Brenil-en-Benoit, in the diocess of Evreux, received a portion, from whence they were afterwards transferred to the abbey of St. Nagloire, at Paris, and from thence to the church of St. Eustachius, in the same city, where they still remain.

But there is reason to doubt their having belonged to St. Agnes, the Roman virgin.—How, indeed, could the city of Utrecht have, in the 10th century, relics of this saint in such quantities as to be able to divide with several churches, when the body of St. Agnes, which was discovered in the 17th century, by cardinal Sfrondrate, appeared entire, with the exception of the head, afterwards found at St. John Lateran as we have already related?

The relics of Utrecht, and consequently all those which have come from this source, belong probably to another St. Agnes, and may, possibly, have come from Rome in the time of the emperor Otho.   There were, in fact, many saints of the same name in Italy.   There was a St. Agnes of Mount Politian, whose feast is celebrated on the 20th of April; an Agnes, sister of St. Clara, who, at Assissium, is often designated as a saint, although the church has not enrolled her among the canonized.   There are others also, whom we might mention, but it appears to us sufficiently established that there could easily have been some confusion between these different saints, bearing the same name.

It is then, at Rome only that the authentic

relics of St. Agnes, virgin and martyr, are offered, with certainty, to the veneration of the catholic world.

END OF THE LIFE OF ST. AGNES.

APPENDIX.

ON THE AUTHENTICITY OF THE ACTS OF ST. AGNES.

The Acts of St. Agnes close by these words:
" I, Ambrose, servant of Christ, have found
these relations in writings little known, and I
have not suffered them to remain any longer
buried in silence. I have, then, published these
Acts, such as I have found them, to the glory
of so illustrious a martyr, and I have thought,
O! virgins of Christ, that the narration of her
martyrdom would serve to your edification, sup-
plicating the charity of the Holy Spirit to cause
that my work may find its fruit in the depth of
your heart, in presence of the Lord."

59

In this Ambrose, servant of Christ, and not
otherwise designated, is naturally, and has been
always understood, the great and holy bishop of
Milan, the only Ambrose known by his writings
in the church. It was, indeed, among his works
that the Acts were at first published by Surius
and afterwards by Bollandus. It seemed to be
indicated, moreover, by the particular venera
tion, which he openly professed for St. Agnes,
whose example he loved to present for the edification of Christian virgins, precisely as is shown
in the Acts.

However, several writers of the two last
centuries have attacked tradition in this respect. But as they bring forward no proof, as
they merely reproduce each other, it is evident
that their assertions come from a common
source. Tracing back then nearer and nearer
to its origin the ground of their attack, we believe it is found in Baronius, to whom many
refer, and before whom we are not aware of any
controversy in this matter.

Baronius says, (speaking of the founding of

the basilica of St. Agnes, by Constantine):
" This fact is related in the following manner
by St. Ambrose, copying an unknown author."
He then quotes the passage of the Acts, and
adds : " It is wrong to give these accounts over
the name of St. Agnes."

We wish particularly, in the first place, to
prove that in the eyes of Baronius himself, the
judgment that he expressed, did no prejudice to
the intrinsic authenticity of the Acts; he was
not ignorant that they reposed upon numerous
and solid proofs ; thus he accepts them as well
established and beyond doubt, since he quotes
these Acts as historical evidence of the foundation of the basilica. Besides it is very clear
that, in speaking of an unknown author, he
refers to the passage of the Acts, which we
have cited, but is easily seen that he stretches
the sense much too far in alleging that they
are falsely attributed to St. Ambrose. For,
indeed the holy bishop of Milan, although he
may not be the author of them, strictly speak-

ing, has none the less given them the authority of his name, in bringing them forth to light.

But if Baronius has stretched the sense of the Acts, the writers, who have followed him, have still more forced or perverted his meaning.

He had said, that the Acts were wrongly recorded over the name of St. Ambrose: Baillet, without further examination, concludes that they are apochryphal and suppositious.

Others, falling into error with regard to the name of Ambrose, which they find concerned in the matter, attribute it, without knowing why, to the unknown author. " We have the Acts, says Tillemont, which may have been written by an Ambrose, but not, indeed, by St. Ambrose of Milan." No! they cannot be by an Ambrose, for this name belongs to him only, who has published, and brought them to light, and if you take him away, there remains but the unknown author, of whose very name we are

Baillet pushes this misunderstanding still further. He even proceeds to make researches as to whom this unknown Ambrose may be, the author of the supposed Acts, and believes he has discovered him in a Greek monk.

But it suffices merely to state these errors, in order to show what value should be put upon the attacks directed against the Acts. They ought, however, by many titles, to be precious and dear to sacred writers; their authenticity is of importance to science as well as religion, and although evidence is wanting for the attacks upon them, numerous proofs are ready to defend them.

We have, in the first place, the hymn of Pru. dentins, a contemporary of St. Ambrose (he was born in 343). It is well known that the verses, of this illustrious poet of the first martyrs, have all the exactness and value of history. Now, the facts related by Prudentius are conformable to the narrative of the Acts; only, we should not be surprised that the latter are more com. plete and give fuller details. for, indeed, a hymn

is not a history and cannot admit of its devel-
opment. But if Prudentius does not refer to
certain particulars, for example, to those which
preceded the martyrdom of St. Agnes, and her
confession of faith ; if he says nothing of the
passion of the prefect's son, nor of those circumstances under which the young virgin was de-
livered up to the judge, and her vow of
virginity made known, does he not seem to
have had these things in view and to have sum-
med them up in the following passage : "She
had, at first, to bear the trial of every kind of
artifice, the brilliant inducements held out in
the flattering speech of the judge, then the
bloody menaces of the executioner."

St. Ambrose himself, in a homily on a book
concerning virgins, and whose authorship this
time has not been contested, evidently makes
allusion to the same facts, when he says:
" What seductions did not the tyrant employ to
gain her over ! What promises did he not
make to win her to his alliance ! But she
replied to him "I pray you injure not my

Spouse by supposing that I could allow myself to be seduced from him by your promises." Is not this precisely the same language that is found in the Acts, and the same order of ideas? And, in a word, because the Acts are more complete than a homily or a hymn, are they entitled to less credit?

But observe that these details, and nearly all those contained in the Acts are confirmed by St. Maximus, bishop of Turin, (in 450) who relates them, exactly in the same manner, in a sermon for the feast of St. Agnes. " Which may," says Baillet, "prove the antiquity of the Acts, since this sermon has been attributed to St. Maximus." What can be thought of such reasoning? Might it not be said, that it is a decided part to reject and deny all proofs, even those collateral to the cause. That the author of this sermon was St. Maximus, has never been questioned, but by Baillet, for there was no reason for it, neither has he any, unless it be that the sermon proves what he denies without proof.

To these written testimonies, a moral proof unites itself, which seems to us of the greatest weight. How can it be admitted that the church, which so carefully collects the particulars of the saints' lives. the Roman church especially, so devoted to St. Agnes, has never had but the apochryphal life and the suppositious Acts of a saint so dear to her—to whom she gave birth, who has always been her glory and her pride; of a saint, in a word, whose praise, St. Jerome tells us, was celebrated among all nations, and all languages? It is clear that, until the time of St. Ambrose (who was born thirty-seven years after the death of St. Agnes) tradition would have sufficed to preserve the details of her life; yet these details were garnered up in ancient writings, which St. Ambrose deemed it expedient to collect and publish. Had he failed to do this, a thousand others would have had like thoughts; a thousand others would have placed her life on record, if it had not been already written in such a man.

ner as to satisfy the spirit of the church and the piety of the faithful.

Thus, let the authorship of the Acts be attributed to St. Ambrose or not; let them have been written by an unknown author, a Greek monk, or by—no matter whom, it is an incontestable fact, that they give the only life of St. Agnes, which tradition has transmitted to us. The church and the faithful having accepted and held this tradition as authentic up to the 16th, or 17th, century, the writers of that epoch had no right to attempt to weaken its authority, at least without bringing proof.

Where is the historical fact, which, on like foundations, would not be received as authentic, and as perfectly established? It is curious to observe the embarrassment of the detractors of the Acts, in the false position in which they have placed themselves. Having taken sides against the truth, they have not sufficient moral courage afterwards to accept it, nor enough boldness and disloyalty openly to disown it. Thus, what an absurd contest is apparent, what desperate efforts of self-love, which would equally defend itself against the truth, which presses it on one side, and against the absurdity, which frightens it on the other.

Baillet sets aside the Acts, it is well understood; but as in them is found nearly the entire life of St. Agnes, and as he cannot suppress all, he is forced to come, from time to time, to borrow from them. It is true that he does so with a very bad grace, we must render him this justice.

"It appears," says he, "that the city of Rome was the theatre of her martyrdom." It appears!—this is amusing! He dares not assume the responsibility of it. It appears, indeed, by other luminous evidence as well as by the Acts, and we would wish to know if it appears otherwise than the greatest personages of history have appeared to exist. It appears, by those infamous places which her presence purified, and of which Rome has made a temple; it appears, by the place of her sepulture on the Numentan road, where so many of the Romans have desired to repose by her side in death; **it** appears again by the famous basilica erected by Constantine. These are material and palpable proofs, without referring to the popular tradition, which has preserved, even to our days, in Rome, the pious veneration of her memory.

It is again in the same doubting style, the same oscillation between the yes and the no that Baillet speaks of the second feast of the 28th of January: "The Church in establishing it, has taken, it seems, for foundation an **uncertain** tradition, but conformable to the Acts of her life, which while little authorized are still quite ancient."

Little authorized! But what more authority does he want than this tradition, which has been perpetuated in the church, and consecrated by the institution of a feast? Thus he prefers supposing error in the church, to admitting truth in the Acts.

Baillet says again: "Her (St. Agnes') beauty caused her to be sought after by many of the first youths of the city, who aspired to a union with her." Where does he find this? The documents, which he denies, say only that she was desired in marriage by the son of the prefect Symphronius. Now where has he found those many suitors of the most noted families of the city? It is his imagination that he follows rather than the Acts, even while he borrows from them the foundation of his narrative.

But, without multiplying quotations of this kind, we can now appreciate the levity of the detractors of the Acts and the value of their arguments.

In the 17th and 18th centuries, several catholic writers allowed themselves to be rashly drawn into like aggressions against the lives of the saints, without foreseeing the fatal consequences of such temerity. Most frequently, we are inclined to think, it was on their part but a question of polemical history, and erudition more less enlightened. But they also subserved, with taking it into considera-

tion, the influence of that new spirit, of that
fatal rationalism, which, since the 16th century, has made so many ravages in the domain
of the church, and even in that of religious
studies and sacred letters, which have the
legends in their possession. These monuments
of the catholic spirit, being no longer defend-
ed by love and the attraction which they formerly inspired, were mutilated with impunity.
When indifference could no longer understand
them, the zeal and enthusiasm, which they had
inspired, became motives for suspicion against
them. It was taken kindly, when their mutila-
tors, who believed themselves doing a pious
work, would lop off the branches regarded as
parasite. How many precious monuments have
thus been weakened, and placed before the
eyes of readers, the generality of whom are
necessarily superficial, and incapable of deep
research. One day, we hope, there will be
found laborious athletes in the halls of science,
who will do justice to this precious inheritance.

A learned Benedictine of our days, F. Guèran ger, abbé of Solesmes, has already done this for the Acts of St. Cecilia, in a profound dis. cussion, which is a model of its kind. But even when a like serious labor shall have been ac- complished with regard to all the Acts, mutila. ted by the hagiographers of the two last cen- turies, the evil caused by their gratuitous conces- sions to rationalism, will not be repaired. They have given it arms, which it will never lay down, while no gratitude is felt for the gift. It is not a breach in the edifice, which it de- mands, but its entire ruin. Rationalism, mean- while has well profited by these concessions: the edifice, pierced through and through, has be- come the object of its laughter, and of suspicion in the public mind. Persons of superficial ac- quirements, in the midst of so many ruins, no longer have confidence in the solidity of that which still remains standing. And what pre- texts have been given to those who are unwill- ing to be weaned from the opinions held by catholic writers, in others respects estimable!

They will accuse the restorers of exaggeration;
rationalism, which still lives, will not accept
this restoration? it will not abandon an inch
of the ground conceded to it, and where
it has established advantageous posts to
attack, what yet remains. But no matter.
the work of restoration must be prosecu.
ted. Christianity is interested in it, for
the lives of the saints is an exposition of the
faith of Christ; they have manifested it by
their works. The Acts of the saints, then, are
like a living Gospel; they are the property, the
riches of the church, our riches also, which we
cannot suffer to be lessened, without losing
some of our inheritance. " The souls of the
saints are in the hands of God," as the Scrip
tures say; he has placed them in glory and beati·
tude, sheltered from every attack, from all
alteration; but their holy relics, and the truths
of their history have been left with us as sacred
deposits. It is to the guardianship of the
church, to the pious veneration of the faithful,
that God has entrusted these precious remains,

which he will, one day, re-establish in glory.- It was the lot of the saints to be persecuted oı earth; the same persecution, which once attack ed their persons, now attacks their memories They were formerly put to death, now they arє denied; it is another way to destroy them. Impiety does not belie herself, she pursues heı work even to the end. Let us also pursue ours, ιet us collect these venerated memories, and en- shrine them in our faith, as the diamond in gold. Let poetry, let the arts surround them with their fascinations; let these awaken senti- ment and affection for them, and when the imagination and the heart are captive, the mind will be more easily convinced. But if ou efforts are powerless to repair these ruins, and restore the Acts of the saints to their origina beauty, God will know how to return to then their imperishable lustre- and what man efface: of their history remains written in heaven.

THE END.

Lightning Source UK Ltd.
Milton Keynes UK
UKHW021844280119
336355UK00027B/1597/P